KITCHENS

KITCHENS

. . . .

A PRACTICAL GUIDE TO DESIGN
AND DECOR FOR YOUR HOME

FAY SWEET

MEREHURST

First published in 1995 by Merehurst Limited,
Ferry House, 51-57 Lacy Road, Putney, London SW15 1PR

ISBN 1 85391 497 5

A catalogue record of this book is available from
the British Library

Designed by Ivor Claydon
Special photography on pages
4, 5, 47, 55, 57, 59 & 61 by Lu Jeffery
Styling by Kate Hardy
Illustrated by Corinne and Ray Burrows

Typesetting by Cameron Typesetting
Colour separation by P & W Graphics, Singapore
Printed in Italy by G. Canale & C., S.p.A

ACKNOWLEDGMENTS

Robert Harding Syndication supplied transparencies on page 7 by Trevor
Richards, Homes & Gardens; page 9 by Jan Baldwin, Homes & Gardens;
page 63 by Steve Hawkins, Ideal Home.
Elizabeth Whiting & Associates supplied transparencies on page 3
by Michael Dunn; pages 4, 31, 32 & 45 by Rodney Hyett; page 49
by Andreas von Einsiedel.
Photography on pages 20, 37, 41 & 43 by Paul Ryan,
International Interiors.
Fay Sweet and the Publishers would like to thank Ikea, The Stencil Store,
Magnet, Tim Wood Furniture, AEG Appliances, Alno Kitchens, Amtico,
Radiating-Style, Fired Earth, Blanco of Germany, CP Hart, Dulux,
Crown Paints, Ecos Paints, & Rösie's Cook Shop.

Contents

Introduction   **page 6**

Section One: Planning and Style
Your Kitchen   **page 8**
Kitchen Planning and Design   **page 14**
Decoration and Use of Colour   **page 24**
Appliances   **page 28**
Lighting   **page 34**
Flooring   **page 36**
The Professional Kitchen   **page 40**

Section Two: The Projects
Tiling the wall behind your work surface   **page 44**
An easy splashback   **page 46**
Painting a wood floor   **page 48**
Storage shelving   **page 50**
Painted doors   **page 52**
Patterning kitchen tiles   **page 54**
Decorative panels for unit doors   **page 56**
A saucepan rack   **page 58**
Storing recyclable materials   **page 60**
New handles   **page 62**

Index   **page 64**

Introduction

The modern kitchen forms the heart of every home. It is a place of warmth, nourishment, hospitality and comforting cooking smells. It is here that we meet for cups of coffee and conversation, or a glass of wine; where we prepare quick snacks, cook favourite meals, experiment with new recipes, and, if we have the room, we share our table with family and friends.

During this century, the design and function of this important room has changed more than any other in the home. Concerns about hygiene and improvements in plumbing have brought about the development of fitted units with continuous, smooth, hardwearing, wipe-clean surfaces. Streamlined, sleek equipment, such as cookers, washing machines and refrigerators, were produced to build in to the standard box units.

This early period of innovation was followed by the development of the labour-saving device. A plethora of electrical gadgets flooded the market to make everything from cake making to clothes washing quicker and easier for the 'busy housewife'. Men, at this stage, rarely ventured into the kitchen.

The latest revolution has concerned itself with ergonomics – making the kitchen a comfortable place in which to work and the environment friendly – making the best use of resources including water and energy. We also find on offer an almost endless choice of fitted or unfitted kitchen styles, and a huge selection of finishes for work surfaces, wall coverings, flooring and lighting.

Essentially, the kitchen has been transformed from a utility space devoted to the preparation and cooking of food for the family, to a comfortable, welcoming, efficient, informal, social room that is now often the focus of our living space.

In this book we have set out to offer practical advice and guidance to help you make the most of your kitchen. You may have recently moved, bought your first home or, perhaps, you would like to give your kitchen a face lift; whatever the case, we hope you will find plenty of design and decorating ideas to inspire and delight you.

The country kitchen has a timeless appeal. The heady blend of natural materials such as wood and slate or ceramic tiles with pretty china and flowers plays on our fondness for nostalgia. The kitchen with a rural feel becomes a comfortable, family room, the heart of the home.

Your Kitchen

Just like successful cooking, the secret of making a perfect kitchen is in the preparation and planning. The first step is to buy a nice thick writing pad and a pencil; a large folder for all the brochures you are sure to collect is also a good idea. Now you are equipped, take a long hard look at your kitchen - its shape, height, size and fittings. Then ask yourself lots of questions.

What sort of space do I have to work with?

The size and plan of your kitchen will play a key role in how it is used; take accurate measurements so that you know exactly what you are dealing with. Measure floor-to-ceiling height as well as length and breadth. Draw a rough plan and mark in doors and windows and the current plumbing arrangements, too. It is always a good idea to have all these measurements to hand when you go shopping as they can help shop staff give you appropriate advice; you never know, you might see the perfect tiles on special offer and you can buy them there and then.

Starting with the very smallest of kitchens, a tiny space is best kept plain and simple unless you delight in chaos. Do not try to cram too much in; it will only make cooking difficult, frustrating and even dangerous.

Remember, a small space does not have to be dull, and it can be fun to use and also extremely efficient. If you have ever taken a holiday on a barge or boat you will know just how little space is actually needed to make a perfectly functional kitchen area. If you have a really small space to work with, it may well prove useful to find and visit companies that supply kitchen fittings for boats.

Another option is to buy one of the kitchen-in-a-box units available on the market. These are the size of a wardrobe and contain an entire mini kitchen. The doors open out to reveal the neat arrangement of stainless steel sink, two-ring hob, refrigerator, coffee maker and a couple of cupboards. One up-market kitchen manufacturer has also devised an all-in-one unit which is a free-standing stainless steel bench incorporating sink, work surface and hob. Both of these compact kitchens can be simply hooked up to the services and can go with you when you move house.

When working with a small area, it is important to make the most of any natural light; it may even be possible to enlarge the window to open up the space more. Removing doors is always a good way of making extra space. Remember, however, you will be obliged in the interests of hygiene and by planning regulations to keep in place any doors separating kitchens and bathrooms. Perhaps knocking down a wall is an option? It may be possible to link the kitchen with the dining room or living room with an arch or widened doorway, or to knock through a large serving hatch.

A medium-sized kitchen, say 3 x 3m (approximately 9 x 9 ft), will have room for a small table or fold-away bar. This sort of space is great for informal suppers but probably not roomy enough for larger dinner parties.

Rustic style on a grand scale. This kitchen with built-in units manages to avoid a clinical look with the clever use of varied textures, natural woods, soft paintwork colours and lots of homely clutter. It is a family space and, as is clear from the glowing array of hanging cooking pans and utensils, it is the source of wonderful meals.

The positioning of doors and windows will have a bearing on where you place units or pieces of furniture. The most useful layouts work on the principal of the sink being linked to the hob/oven on the longest, unbroken stretch of work surface. This gives you a large area for food preparation and for stacking crockery for washing. The refrigerator can be located further away.

Is the sink in the most useful place? Traditionally it is sited under the window for ease of plumbing and to give the sink user an outside view. However, you may prefer to plumb in a dishwasher and put your table by the window? Would this mean an expensive re-plumbing job?

The large kitchen is one of the most difficult to plan. The temptation, if you can afford it, is to fit in yards of units, but perhaps you do not really need so many. It may suit you very well to keep the working part of your kitchen small and contained at one end or corner of the room so that the rest of the space can be given over to a large table.

Another option is to build in an island unit. This acts as a sort of work station and can be the place for a large, uninterrupted work surface or perhaps also incorporate a hob and/or sink.

How do I want to use this space?

First of all you should think carefully about your life-style and the sort of cooking you have time for and enjoy. If you are not particularly interested, or have a demanding job that leaves limited time for cooking or entertaining, there is little to be gained by spending huge sums of money on an expensive fitted kitchen and lorry loads of the latest cookers, food processors and a host of other gadgets. Your efforts will probably be best spent smartening up the room with a coat of fresh paint, a good-quality fridge-freezer to store prepared foods and a microwave oven.

For those who like informal meals shared with family and friends, finding room for a table should be a priority. There are few evenings more enjoyable than those spent sitting around a candle-lit table with congenial company. If space is limited, perhaps a couple of under-used units can be sacrificed to make more room for your table.

If, however, you like to entertain on a grand scale, you may prefer to keep guests at bay in another room. Unless you are extremely relaxed, having friends rifling through drawers to find the bottle opener can be intensely annoying when you are putting the final touches to the hollandaise sauce! If you cook regularly then you are likely to want plenty of room for fresh ingredients.

If you have young children, you will be faced with a completely different set of needs. No matter how large your home, the kitchen will act as a magnet for all sorts of activities. Children will want to help with the cooking, play games and use the table for drawing, colouring and homework. The essential here is a rugged, serviceable table. For your own peace of mind, forget about anything with a finely-polished surface - there are sure to be spills and scratches and the odd slip of the pens and crayons. A good solid pine top that is easy to scrub clean will save a lot of heartache. Storage for toys and games is also worth considering. A simple chest or small cupboard should do the trick.

At this early stage it is also valuable to consider the needs of elderly or disabled friends and family members and to try and incorporate them in your plans; for example, ramps can

All manner of ingenious devices have been dreamed up by fitted kitchen designers. Here we show a cooler fitted with drawers that are ideal for storing vegetables and dairy produce. The unit is designed to slot neatly into a run of standard size fitted cupboards.

replace steps and wide doorways will allow room for wheelchairs.

What do I like and dislike?

Here is the opportunity for some very satisfying list making. You might not be able to afford all the things you like at once but, by making a list, you should be able to identify the priorities. The secret of success here is not just to take a look at your present kitchen, but also to remember what you liked and disliked about your last kitchen, and those of others.

A good place to start is style. Do you prefer fitted kitchens to those furnished with free-standing furniture? It would be a great waste to rip out and throw away perfectly good carcasses if you can achieve a face-lift simply by painting or changing the doors. If you are aiming for a rustic look, then try plain pine; if you want something a little more bright and streamlined, there are plenty of smooth-finished melamine-faced doors available in a huge choice of colours. It is also worth remembering that it is a fairly straightforward task to dismantle the collection of units you may have inherited and re-configure them to suit your needs.

Think of colour schemes, too. If you have a dark kitchen you might like to transform it into a light, white space, or you could play on the darkness and turn it into an intriguing cavern. Perhaps you have some favourite china, coloured cooking pots or collection of jugs that you would like to build a colour scheme around?

Once the storage areas are decided, you can think about work tops. Solid wood looks wonderful but, to prevent warping and splitting, it often requires maintenance. Stones such as marble and granite also look fabulous; they have the added benefit of needing little attention to keep them looking good, but they can be astronomically expensive. A slightly less expensive option here is terrazzo - a composite of stone fragments. Ceramic tiles are hardwearing and can look superb; however, these can look ugly if not laid properly and the grouting has a tendency to stain. One of the least expensive and toughest options is laminate. This is available in many colours and patterns and is virtually indestructible.

Next to consider are wall coverings and floorings. There is a huge choice available (see page 36). In the meantime, think carefully about your require-ments; ceramic floor tiles may look great, but they can be cold to walk on - would vinyl be better?

Lighting can be extremely difficult to get right (see page 34). Ask yourself whether you like side lighting or a central pendant, working in bright light or a slightly muted glow?

Finally in this section, consider what sort of kitchen appliances you like to use. If you have the option, do you prefer cooking by gas or electricity? Do you like floor or wall-mounted ovens? Is a dishwasher a good idea?

What can I achieve within my budget?

Be absolutely realistic about what you can afford. Build in an emergency fund of ten per cent for the unexpected. If you are planning to live with this kitchen for a short time, do not be tempted to spend a fortune. Finally, make yourself the promise that you will shop around and compare prices. Always aim to collect three quotes for any work and never take the first you are offered.

The use of white gives a kitchen a clean, fresh look. The central, free-standing hob inset into a work-surface makes an unusual feature. The idea of adding a central island adds interest to the large room and provides a bench for informal eating and drinking.

Kitchen Planning and Design

There is no end of advice available on kitchen design; however, essentially, what we all want is a kitchen that functions well for our needs, that has adequate and convenient storage space, that is comfortable to work in and, of course, that looks good.

When starting your design, remember to refer to your notes on how you want to use the space and your likes and dislikes. It is important at this early stage to build in consideration for those who are very tall or very short and for kitchen users who may have disabilities and special needs. Fitted kitchen manufacturers produce units in standard sizes are based on a module that is 60cm wide x 60cm deep x 90cm high (24 in wide x 24 in deep x 36 in high). While many variations of width and depth are available, few offer different height options. If you are very tall, one solution to the height problem is to raise the entire fitted kitchen on blocks; if you are short, you could remove part of the base to lower the overall height. The disadvantage of tailoring your kitchen so specifically is that when you come to move, prospective buyers may take exception to your alterations.

To help you in your planning and design we discuss here the five classic kitchen shapes and how to make the most of your available space.

The U-Shaped Kitchen

This is an extremely practical layout to work with as you are likely to have just one doorway interrupting your plan. If you choose to fit units, this shape offers the opportunity for a continuous run of work surface round most of the room. Even the tiniest spaces perform well as everything will be within easy reach.

The classic layout for this type of kitchen is to place tall items such as an upright fridge-freezer at one end of the 'U' and, at the other, a broom storage cupboard or wall-fixed oven. If you opt for this layout, and you have a door opening into the space, ensure that there is sufficient clearance for the door to swing open without crashing into you as you carry food in and out of refrigerator or oven. The ideal solution is to make the door outward opening, fit a space-saving sliding door or to remove it altogether.

To make good use of all the space, and to slightly soften the room's angularity, you may like to set the hob/oven or sink across the corner. Triangular shaped sinks are designed for this purpose. In a narrow U-shaped room, ensure that there is plenty of space to open fridge and oven doors without bumping into units behind.

The L-Shaped Kitchen

If the room is very large, you may opt to arrange your units and appliances along just two walls to form an L-shaped work area. This design will cut the walking distance between sink,

This handsome, free-standing storage unit serves many useful functions. It has plenty of room for displaying attractive dishes, and in the two end piers there is space to stow linen, candlesticks and other dining items. The unit also acts as a room divider to screen off the dining area.

refrigerator and cooker and should leave space for a table opposite.

This layout works well in both large and narrow rooms. As mentioned above, in a large room you will have space to fit units and appliances along two walls and have room left for a table. If the space allows, you might even add a counter to one end of the 'L', to enclose the food preparation and cooking area and separate it from the eating area. The counter could also function as an eating bar.

The Galley Kitchen

This is the name usually applied to kitchens shoe-horned into a tiny space with a door or opening at either end. This passage-like arrangement has the disadvantage of being walk through; however, good planning will make the best use of your space. An efficient layout plan places the sink and cooker/hob on one side of the room, preferably served by natural light from a window, with the refrigerator opposite.

The Line Kitchen

I have seen a variety of line kitchen arrangements, ranging from those in large kitchen/dining rooms to others in little more than a wide corridor.

The line arrangement enforces great design discipline. Keep the central section or work surface as uninterrupted as possible. A completely workable plan is to start with a small area of work surface, followed by hob/oven or cooker, then the longest stretch of surface, completed by the sink and draining board. The fridge can be placed anywhere in the line.

The Island Kitchen

This really only works when you have the luxury of plenty of floor area. The 'island' can consist of a block of storage units with a plain work surface, or the central block can incorporate a hob and/or sink. The size of your budget is important when considering the second option, as you will face the additional plumbing costs of running the services - water, electricity and/or gas - through or beneath the floor. A central hob may also require an overhead extractor fan.

The ultimate in sleek chic. This blonde wood fitted kitchen with its smooth surfaces and minimal accessories is extremely neat. This single wall of units contains all the electrical appliances you'd find in much larger rooms and with the floor-to-ceiling fitted units, there is a surprisingly generous amount of storage space.

Central islands also offer the option of two different work heights recommended by the ergonomics experts; the regular height is good for general food preparation and a slightly lower level is ideal for pastry rolling and dough kneading which requires more muscular effort.

The Work Triangle

When you start to draw up a layout plan you will come across the phrase 'the work triangle'. This is the design concept commonly used to ensure the kitchen is easy and comfortable in which to work. It means that the sink, hob/oven and refrigerator will form the points of your triangle.

The key to success is to have an uninterrupted work area running between sink and hob/cooker. The ideal length is somewhere around one or two metres. Less than one metre and you will feel cramped; longer than two and you will be wasting time and energy moving around the space. The refrigerator position is the most flexible of the triangle. Ideally, for convenience, that too should be within a couple of metres of sink and hob.

The shape of your room and the position of windows and doors will, in part, dictate how you should plan your layout. Take time to stand back and consider all your options. Does the room have any intriguing architectural details that you can emphasise or enhance? Perhaps there is an interesting chimney breast nook that can be used to frame or display a small piece of sculpture or beautiful jug? Can the cornice be picked out in a colour contrasting with the rest of the room? Perhaps the style of window can be echoed in glass-fronted cupboards? Any major structural work will, of course, add to your budget. However, even fairly inexpensive alterations can pay huge dividends in making your kitchen an easier or pleasanter place in which to work. It is well worth seeking professional advice and asking for a few quotes to discover how much or little you may need to spend.

The sink and cooker positions are the first to decide upon. The old school of design always placed the sink under the window - the thinking behind this was that you will spend a large proportion of your time standing at the sink and will want a view out. It also made - and, indeed, still makes - sound sense to run plumbing along the outside wall. Today, however, we may prefer to make the most of the window's natural light by having it fall on a work surface or on a table. Dining at a table with a view can be infinitely preferable to washing up with a view.

Once you have selected the ideal position for the sink, try and fix the cooker or hob nearby. If possible, allow for an area of work surface on both side of the hob, providing space for resting saucepans. The length of surface between sink and hob should be generous enough to provide space for food preparation and for stacking washing up. Avoid siting a hob, oven or cooker near a doorway - it can be extremely dangerous.

As long as you do not place the refrigerator close to an inward-opening door, it can stand almost anywhere in the room. If the refrigerator door has fixed hinges, ensure you can open it easily and safely.

Now you have worked out your basic work triangle, you can plan the rest of your storage and work space.

A small space skilfully handled. Most of the functioning part of this kitchen is built into the recess beside the door, while the flat-top cooking hob has been brought to the middle of the room where it acts as a divider, separating the food preparation area from the dining area. Colour, of course, plays a large role in adding interest to the space.

Storage

Most people opt for a fitted kitchen to maximise the potential space for storage. However, the unfitted or non-kitchen look can make a welcome and refreshing alternative.

The design of the fitted kitchen has become incredibly sophisticated and the clever storage ideas are endless. Look out for devices such as sliding, pull-out larders, fold-away ironing boards and corner cupboards with a swivel rack.

In the unfitted kitchen, the pine dresser has traditionally provided the ideal space for storage and display but, for something a little more unusual, how about using a wooden wardrobe? Painted or plain wood, and fitted with shelves, a wardrobe is a great storage unit. Bookcases and shop display cabinets, too, can make an excellent and practical storage spaces, which can be loaded with wine bottles, attractive jars and cookery

The unfitted kitchen has a great deal of charm. For a unified look, select pieces made of the same or similar material — in this case a rich, honey pine. The dresser has been a favourite item of kitchen furniture for centuries — it is extremely practical for storage and has plenty of space for displaying special items.

books. With a little imagination, there is no limit to the types of furniture you can introduce to an unfitted kitchen - even an old office filing cabinet or chest of drawers can make the perfect place to store saucepans and baking trays.

Shelving, as an alternative to fitted top cupboards, gives the kitchen a lighter, more open feel. Shelves also provide an opportunity to create an attractive display with jars, bottles, glasses or crockery. There are many types of shelving units and shelving kits available on the market but, if you want to try something unusual, consider using thick-gauge industrial glass, marble, concrete, bricks or stainless steel. The free-standing stainless steel shelving units designed for professional kitchens can look extremely elegant loaded with stainless steel saucepans and kitchen equipment. Saucepans, large dishes and cooking utensils may, alternatively, be stored on a trolley. Given a wooden or marble top this could also double as a work surface.

Hanging rails and racks are becoming increasingly popular - especially for storing bulky items such as saucepans - and are ideal for small kitchens. Avoid any temptation to hang saucepans close to your hob as

they will soon become greasy and dusty.

A number of manufacturers have produced wood and stainless steel rails and racks, many of which are available with accessories such as clip-on trays for holding kitchen roll. A less expensive alternative is to fix a simple wooden broom handle or towel rail to your kitchen wall (see page 00). Wall-hung plate racks are excellent too and allow you to keep everyday crockery within easy reach. When fixed above the sink they can double as a drainer.

In any kitchen, whether fitted or not, it is possible to work out a logical sequence of storage. Essentially, those things used most often should be stored close at hand, with the rule that the less frequently an item is used, the more distant it can be. It is wise to try to make sure that all objects are fairly easily accessible. A tightly-packed cupboard is extremely uninviting and the prospect of sorting through for a well-buried plate is so daunting that it will probably stay there for ever, gathering dust.

Classic storage plans place either vegetable racks or waste bins, bin bags and cleaning materials under the sink. An alternative store for cleaning materials is a tall cupboard where you may also store a broom and ironing board.

Cupboards and shelves above the sink should be used for light and small items, such as mugs, glasses, measuring jugs, tea and coffee pots, crockery, and dried, tinned and bottled foods.

Heavy items, such as saucepans, casserole dishes, food processors and so on, should be stored in base units. Placed high up they become difficult to lift up and down and could cause injury if they fall. If you have a dining table in the kitchen it is a good idea to store crockery, cutlery and glasses in the nearest cupboard or shelf unit.

A one-drawer unit is always useful for cutlery, table linen and small items of kitchen equipment.

Finishes for Cupboards and Work Tops

The finishes you choose will set the style of your kitchen. As a guide, if you want to create a warm, comfortable feel then choose from a palette of natural materials, particularly woods. For an efficient, hygienic style of kitchen, select smooth-finish laminates; for the professional look buy stainless steel.

To transform old kitchen cupboards, it is now possible to buy and fit new doors (see pages 56-7). As long as your cupboards are sound and of a standard size, this can save a great deal of unnecessary expense and wasted materials in buying entirely new units. You can even achieve a bit of a face lift simply by replacing old handles.

Think carefully about your colour choice. Dark shades, such as plum, bottle green and navy blue, will look cosy and inviting, while pale tones will reflect more light and open out the room.

Texture is extremely important too. Unit doors with panels, wood and stone and terracotta textures make a charming, rustic-style room; while smooth, laminates and steel and ceramic look distinctly urban and chic.

Work tops are available in dozens of materials, textures and patterns. One of the most popular, practical and least expensive is laminate. This man-made material copes well with the wear and tear of kitchen life, as it is tough, waterproof, hygienic, scratch and heat resistant.

More expensive man-made materials include Corian, a type of artificial stone. Like

laminate, it is hardwearing, easily wiped clean, water and heat resistant. Unlike laminate, it is a solid material that can be cut and shaped to provide a smooth and seamless surface.

Woods, such as beech and maple, have an enduring appeal and are easily cut to the required size and shape. When oiled or varnished they are water resistant, but require occasional maintenance to keep them looking good. If well cared for, wood can improve with age. Always check the source of the wood you are buying - imported hardwoods may have been cut from rain forests or other unsustainable sources. Reputable suppliers will know where the wood has been grown.

Ceramic tiles are relatively inexpensive and hardwearing. However, they are prone to cracking and suffer from the problem of grubby grout. Water-resistant grout is available but this may stain. When staining is severe it is best to dig out old grout and replace with new.

Stainless steel is the choice of the professional chef. It is durable, hygienic, easily cleaned, and heat and stain resistant. It will scratch, but this gives the material a charming patina.

Stones such as marble, granite and slate, are heat and stain resistant and, although they can sometimes chip, are generally very hardwearing; on the down side, they are also extremely expensive.

Safety and Comfort Tips

The kitchen is the most dangerous place in the home. There are dozens of opportunities to cut and scald and bruise yourself, so always bear safety in mind when making your plans.

• Make sure inward-opening doors do not crash into you while you are working. Change the hinges to make the door swing outwards, fit a sliding door or remove it altogether.

• Do not hang anything flammable, such as curtains, dried flowers or wooden spoons, near a gas flame. This warning applies to boiler pilot lights as well as gas hob rings.

• Ensure your kitchen is well ventilated. Gas appliances require adequate ventilation by law.

• If you choose to hang an airing rack or saucepan rail from the ceiling, ensure there is plenty of headroom underneath. Make sure there is enough to spare even the tallest of guests from knocking themselves out on your favourite copper saucepan.

• Avoid storing heavy items, such as large cooking pots, jugs, vases, bowls or food processors, at the top of cupboards. They will

be difficult and dangerous to remove.

• Always try and plan for a generous area of work surface at the side of cooker where you can put hot saucepans and pots safely when removed from the heat.

• Install plenty of electric sockets in your kitchen. This reduces the opportunity of trailing dangerous cable across work surfaces.

• Never trail electrical cable across a cooker, hob or sink.

• Consider finishing a run of units with a rounded end unit. This is a particularly good idea in a small kitchen as it will prevent bumping into sharp corners.

• Install a fire blanket and fire extinguisher.

• Leave a margin for error in units that must house appliances such as a washing machine or dishwasher. They are incredibly heavy and can be difficult to remove for repair if they fit too tightly.

• When designing lighting, ensure the light is cast directly on to the work surface and not on to you as this will cast shadows.

• If you have young children, fit a guard rail on to your hob to stop them reaching saucepans.

Fitted kitchen suppliers, such as Magnet in the UK, are happy to draw up plans of your kitchen to suggest different layouts and positions for a variety of units. This computer-generated example of a galley kitchen demonstrates how to maximise the use of space both at the ground level and on the walls.

Decoration and Use of Colour

Since most of your kitchen wall space will be taken up with cupboards and appliances, there may only be a small area of wall left to decorate. However, by paying careful attention to the detail you will make the most of the whole.

Wall Coverings

Ceramic Tiles One of the most popular kitchen wall finishes, these are available in a huge variety of colours and patterns, are easy to fix, relatively inexpensive and offer a durable, stain-resistant, bright, easy to clean, surface. The main drawback with ceramic tiles is that the grout tends to become grubby and stained. It can be scrubbed to remove the worst of the gathered dirt but, if stains persist, it is advisable to scrape out old grout and replace it with new. If tiles are placed in areas likely to be exposed to great heat, condensation, oil or water splashes, ensure you fix them with a water-resistant grout.

Tiles most usually appear in a horizontal band, two or three tiles deep, behind the work surface where they act as a splash back and as protection from knocks and scratches (see page 44). They can also look stunning fixed on the entire height of the wall to ceiling level. Mosaics, many of which are sold in ready-assembled panels, are unusual and stylish.

Paint and paint effects The most versatile of all finishes, paint is often all that is needed to transform a kitchen from a dowdy , depressing place to a jolly one. In areas that require regular cleaning, such as behind a cooker, or that are exposed to water splashes, such as behind a sink, oil-based mixtures are often the best choice. They will withstand more wear and tear and washing down than water-based products.

Many manufacturers concerned about environment-damaging ingredients have now formulated eco-friendly blends. These solvent-free paints incorporate natural raw materials such as linseed oil, pine resin, chalk and essential oils. They are pleasant to use and are particularly recommended for asthma and allergy sufferers.

If you are feeling adventurous, you could try a mural or any one of the many paint effects that are easily accomplished. Rag-rolling, sponging and dragging have become rather over-used; however, stippling is a delicate and intriguing finish - special stippling brushes can be bought from most good paint stores. Amongst the most popular of paint decoration effects is stencilling. There are numerous specialist companies producing a vast array of stencil designs, complete with full instructions.

Wallpaper This generally only works well in large kitchens with a separate dining area. In a small kitchen, hanging wallpaper behind and round units can be a complete nightmare. You will also find that, unless you splash out on an expensive vinyl paper, the finish will not withstand the wear and tear of a busy kitchen and will soon become scruffy. However, if you do have the

Green tiles and white kitchen units combine to make a fresh and crisp kitchen colour scheme. The effect is heightened with accessories in stainless steel. The dazzling brightness is brought down to earth by the wood floor. A pale floor covering could have made the room feel unwelcoming.

luxury of space for a dining area, wallpaper could provide the perfect solution to marking this off from the cooking area.

Wood Many DIY stores now stock wood panelling kits. You can opt for square panels or a tongue-and-groove style. This sort of finish works well when fixed from floor to work surface height to give you a half-panelled room. The wood is usually sold unfinished so you can varnish or paint it.

Stainless steel
Not frequently seen in domestic kitchens, behind work surfaces, cookers and sinks, stainless steel makes an ideal splash back. It is easy to fix (see pages 46-7), inexpensive, extremely durable, easy to clean, stylish and can be used to disguise uneven or damaged walls.

Perspex If you are not fond of ceramic tiles, this tough, hygienic sheet material makes an ideal splash back. It is available in a wide range of colours but, in its clear form, it can be fixed over a painted wall so you still see the paint colour, with added protection against knocks and splashes.

Colour Schemes

By the time you come to decorate your walls, you will certainly have thought long and hard about colour schemes. You will have made some decisions already by choosing the units and furniture for the space.

Personal preference and association are powerful ingredients in making your choice. A very good idea is to build a scheme around a collection of crockery, a favourite painting or poster, or a theme such as the country kitchen or the Mediterranean kitchen.

In practical terms, you should take into account the colours of the units and furniture already chosen. Blues, yellows and white look wonderful with wood finishes, a pewter colour looks chic with stainless steel, garlic pink looks great with wood and steel, and so on. Also take note of the amount, quality and timing of natural light that floods the room. North-facing rooms receive little or no direct sunlight, east-windows receive the weak morning sun, west-facing rooms get the rich evening light and south-facing will receive direct sunlight through most of the day. To warm up the feel of a room, choose from the red end of the spectrum; to produce a cooling effect, use blues and greens.

It is interesting to note that colours can have a strong psychological and even physical effect on us. Reds have been shown to quicken the heartbeat, increase blood pressure and stimulate taste buds (the reason why so many restaurants are decorated using red); blues have the opposite effect. Virulent limey greens make people feel uncomfortable (in experiments, when used in company washrooms, lime green walls dramatically reduced the time people spent there), and pinks can be calming (pink shades have been used in prison cells to quieten aggressive inmates).

As a general rule when choosing paint, light colours will open out a space and dark will close it in. Picking out woodwork in a colour that is darker than the walls will draw attention to those details and give emphasis.

An ill-lit room may look at its best simply decorated in white. White does, in fact, suit almost every kitchen because of its associations with cleanliness and purity. Breaking the rules can produce successful results too - for example, a rich navy blue or emerald green, or the two together, can look fabulous in tiny spaces and gives the effect of a glinting jewel box.

The classic combination of red and green is shown to dramatic effect in this light and spacious kitchen. The darkness of the units is offset by the pale wallpaper, the stripped door and wood table. Red and green accessories continue the theme.

Appliances

If you are planning to spend seriously large amounts of money on your kitchen, you will have no problem at all finding expensive, de luxe, multi-functional, super-efficient appliances sporting control panels bristling with so many buttons, dials and displays they would look completely at home in the cockpit of a jumbo jet. However, back down on earth, the rest of us are more likely to be looking for good quality, efficiency and value for money. Whatever the size of your budget, there is plenty of choice.

Of growing concern in this area is the production of machines that are environment friendly. Many have been designed and developed to maximise efficiency and use less water, less detergent, less energy than previous models. Many kitchen appliance manufacturers have taken the green message extremely seriously and now package their goods in environment-friendly, recycled and recyclable materials, finish them with low-solvent or solvent-free paints, and design machines in such a way that makes it possible to recycle components easily at the end of the appliance's useful life.

Cookers, Ovens, Hobs and Microwaves

The first consideration when buying any sort of cooking appliance is the fuel you intend to use. Solid fuel (wood and coal) is the least convenient and is rarely used in towns or cities, whereas electricity and gas are clean, efficient and available just about everywhere - although it is worth noting that a gas mains supply can be difficult to come by in rural areas. If you have access to both the main fuels, the most popular cooking combination is a gas hob, ideal for instant heat and precise control, and an electric oven. Fan ovens are the most energy efficient as they circulate hot air continuously to cook faster.

Decide just how much and what style of cooking you are likely to undertake. For example, if you are not very interested in cooking and prefer convenience or prepared meals, then a microwave oven and a standard, no-frills oven will be all you need. If, however, you have the time for, and interest in, more traditional methods of cooking, you will opt for a standard cooker. For the real enthusiast, there is also the option of a free-standing professional-style cooker. While these are a joy to cook with, they are extremely expensive. Where space is at a premium, compact ovens and two-ring hobs are now available.

The styles of cookers and ovens include free-standing units incorporating oven, hob and perhaps also a separate grill, and, with the same sort of functions, slide-in machines designed to slot in to a space between fitted units. These are a considerably less expensive option to installing separate oven and hob. In addition, there are many styles of in-built appliances: single and double ovens that fit under work tops and others, perhaps combining

Corners are often considered dead space and places where unnecessary clutter can accumulate. However, imaginative planning and design has made good use of the corner space in this kitchen as the site for the cooker, hob and extractor hood.

a large and small oven or microwave and grill, designed to fit in a tall unit that stretches between floor and ceiling. This latter design is an expensive option because of the housing unit cost, but is excellent for those with back problems or physical disabilities as it eliminates the need for bending down to remove hot dishes from the oven. If your kitchen is being designed with the elderly or disabled in mind, always ensure that controls on appliances are easy to turn on and off and are clear and easy to read. Also, for safety and to prevent burning, it is important to check that oven doors are well insulated and remain cool when in use.

Other considerations include the fact that ovens with an integral grill can prove annoying, as you will not be able to roast and grill at the same time. In addition, the grill elements can become spotted with grease from roasting meats and smoke very badly when first switched on. Take note of the way an oven door opens, with a left, right or bottom hinge? The left- and right-hinged types require less opening space, which may be more convenient for small or narrow kitchens.

If you are installing a separate oven and hob, your choice of hob will depend on the type of cooking fuel you require and your budget. They are available as gas, electric or gas and electric combined, and in a wide variety of finishes from white, black or brown enamel to stainless steel. With fitted kitchens there is no necessity to have hob and oven close to each other and this allows for flexibility of layout. You may find it convenient, for example, to fit the hob along the same work surface as the sink and choose to place the oven in a wall unit elsewhere in the kitchen. The most modern and expensive hobs are the smooth-surfaced ceramic variety; they glow when hot and are easily wiped clean. Among the latest hob innovations are touch-sensitive controls and electric halogen light elements - these allow you to cook using light which heats and cools in seconds.

The microwave oven, with its ability to defrost, heat and cook foods, has found favour in countless kitchens. Many people find them invaluable for cooking prepared or frozen meals at the end of a busy day. Sophisticated versions of the microwave are described as combination ovens. These incorporate a grill and fan to brown foods and cook them in a conventional way. The machines have the advantage of being quick to use, economical to run, easy to accommodate even in the smallest of kitchens, and easy to clean.

Extractor Fans

The favourite choice of extractor is the type that is fitted above the hob and enclosed in a cooker hood. You will be offered the choice between those that draw the air away from the cooking area and expel it outside and others that take air through a filter and re-circulate it in the room. The first is usually the most efficient and works best when cooker and hood are fitted on an outside wall, keeping the distance of ducting to a minimum.

One of the most common complaints voiced about extractor fans is the whirring noise they make. This problem can sometimes be solved quickly and simply by replacing or cleaning the filter, which may have become clogged by grease. Another, more expensive, solution is to fit a larger or more powerful extractor. Check the manufacturer's instructions to see what capacity extractor is recommended for the size of your kitchen. Troublesome extractors are generally those that must struggle for a long time to clean the air of a room larger than they are intended to serve.

Refrigerators and Freezers

Once again, your life-style and level of interest in cooking will dictate what sort of refrigerator and/or freezer you buy. If there are just two of you in the home and you do not cook often, a refrigerator to fit under a work surface with an integral freezer compartment may be all you need. Those who cook frequently will need a large refrigerator for storing fresh produce - large salad drawers are essential. If you use a lot of convenience and frozen foods, you will need a larger freezer section and may opt for an upright unit which is half refrigerator, half freezer. Horizontal fridge-freezers are also very useful as they can slot under a work surface or a counter top.

Unless you have a large family, beware of buying a large freezer. You could find that you are storing goods unnecessarily, and at considerable expense, for months and even years. Very small and slim-line refrigerators and freezers are available for tiny kitchens.

Before buying your refrigerator or freezer, check which way its doors open. If they are wrong for you, ask if they can be changed round - many appliances now offer this

option. You may also want a unit that allows you to fix a decor panel to the door, enabling you to put a panel on the refrigerator door that matches the other doors in a fitted kitchen.

Dishwashers

Great strides have been made in improving the performance, energy, water and detergent consumption of dishwashers

For those who really love cooking it is worth setting aside a portion of your budget for a really good cooker and hob. This combination of appliances – a hob with five rings and a capacious oven – is ideal for those with a big family or who enjoy large dinner parties. The stainless steel splashback is smart and practical.

since they first arrived on the scene. Indeed, many are now so efficient that manufacturers claim they can save at least forty per cent of the cost of washing up by hand.

The best designs incorporate good insulation allowing them to operate much more quietly than ever before. Noise and vibration can be reduced yet further by setting the appliance on a rubber mat. They should also include an anti-flood device, easy running trays, and good filtration to keep clean water in circulation.

Washing Machines

Machines are designed either as top loading or front loading - the latter is ideal for slotting under a kitchen work surface. They are also are sold in styles that will allow you to fix a decor panel to match the rest of your kitchen units.

Unless you have access to, or like to use, outdoor space for drying, it is best to buy an integrated washer-dryer. If you

For the really serious cook, there are few appliances to beat the Aga-style cooker. The French machine pictured features two electric ovens, a four-ring gas hob and a large gas-fired griddle. This is virtually a professional standard appliance.

have plenty of space, a separate washing machine and tumble dryer may be considered. These can stand side by side or one on top of the other.

Sinks and Waste Disposal

The humble kitchen sink is no longer so humble. There is now the option to use it with accessories such as an integrated chopping board, waste chute, colander basket, vegetable and salad washer, plate rack, and retractable spray hose.

If you have plenty of space, a good-sized, straightforward, double-bowl sink with draining board is ideal, as you will have space for washing and rinsing and draining. If you are a keen cook, buy the largest sink possible - there will always be a large roasting tray, fish kettle or pasta saucepan that demands your personal attention. In more restricted areas one-and-a-half bowls plus drainer serves well and triangular, corner-fitting sinks make good use of awkward space. Before buying any sink, ensure that it will be compatible with your fitted units; very deep models may not be suitable for some systems.

It is a good idea to decide at the kitchen planning stage whether or not you would like and can afford a waste disposal unit, as it

is easiest to fit them alongside the rest of the plumbing work. Some manufacturers also offer waste chutes that allow you to dispose of compost-type waste matter, such as fruit and vegetable trimmings, through a neat trap set into the work surface that leads to a compost bin.

Sinks are now offered in a range of materials. The old-fashioned, deep, rectangular fired clay or ceramic variety have become very popular; however, they can look awkward with modern fitted units. There are also several varieties of plastics; the ones with slightly textured finishes can wear badly as they have a tendency to stain. Very new on the scene are the stone and resin composite sinks. These look extremely elegant with a speckled finish that is durable, heat, stain and acid resistant.

Few materials have surpassed stainless steel, which is pressed from a sheet and so has no joins in which germs and dirt can be harboured. It also wears extremely well. Stainless steel comes in a variety of thicknesses; buy the thickest gauge possible.

Your choice of taps is likely to be based on personal preference: mixer or individual, fixed or swivel taps, stainless steel or brass. Before buying, make sure your taps and sink are compatible.

Lighting

Lighting can make or break a room. It can also create or ruin a mood. Glaring lights will literally put you in the spotlight and will generate a feeling of unease. Insufficient lighting will cast a shadow of gloom over the room, making it unwelcoming and dowdy. The perfect balance is achieved by installing general room lighting, either ceiling or wall-fixed, and good, crisp lighting over work areas (this is called task lighting).

The lighting you choose should be sympathetic to the kitchen decor and the ways in which you use the room. A pine-based kitchen will look cosy and homely with table lamps, while a modern-style, windowless galley kitchen is likely to suit sparkly low-voltage halogen contemporary fittings.

Working with electricity involves a great deal of potential danger and fitting new lights is a skilled job. Unless you are entirely competent, it is highly recommended that you employ an expert. Always check on fittings for the recommended maximum bulb wattage - if this is exceeded, you may cause damage to the lamp.

Types of Light

Tungsten This is the light provided by regular domestic bulbs. The clear bulb will cast a warm, slightly yellow light. In addition, there are many pearl-finished and coloured bulbs now available on the market. Tungsten strips are also sold.

Fluorescent This is most commonly used as strip lighting. Fluorescent tubes are available in a wide variety of lengths; they are long lasting and energy efficient and therefore cheap to run. Due to its blue-white colour, fluorescent is rather harsh on the eye and should ideally be fixed behind a shield, a cupboard pelmet for example.

Halogen The low-voltage halogen light has become increasingly popular in recent years because it emits a wonderful, crisp, white, sparkling light. The drawbacks are that lights must be fitted with transformers and that the bulbs themselves, while long lasting if treated with care, are fragile and expensive.

Designing Your Lighting Scheme

When you start to design your kitchen lighting scheme, bear in mind both practical and aesthetic considerations. The first is to ensure that you have adequate and practical light in which to work; to avoid shadows, make sure the light is cast directly on your work top and not on you. The second is related to 'painting' your space with light; you may wish to highlight certain areas and play down others.

Most rooms have a central, ceiling-suspended pendant which takes a tungsten bulb. This is a start, but, even with an attractive shade, the effect is often stark and utilitarian in feel. Pendant lighting also casts shadows and has a tendency to give the effect of lowering ceiling heights. Depending on your taste, a central light can be supplemented by wall-fixed lights (these should be placed above eye-level to give a gentle, inviting glow), or perhaps a couple of ever-versatile table lamps. Dimmer switches are more expensive than regular controls, but they are an extremely good investment as they allow great flexibility. Other options include converting your central pendant into a rise-and-fall lamp that can be brought down to illuminate a dining table, island work surface or counter, and then lifted out of the way when not required.

Alternatively, track lighting could be installed with several spotlights which can be angled to wherever they are most needed. Recessed lighting is also effective and flexible. These fittings are set into the ceiling and can be positioned directly over work surfaces or, if they are the sort with a moveable 'eyeball' centre, can be used as wall washers or to highlight specific objects or areas. Recessed lamps are particularly useful in rooms with low ceilings - you will not need to duck under the bulbs.

If you have a high ceiling, an excellent way of throwing light upwards is to fix small up-lighters above wall-fixed units or on high shelves. Light will bounce off the ceiling and fall as a soft glow.

The secret of using fluorescent effectively is to conceal the tubes behind the pelmet or baffle at the bottom of wall units. The pelmet shields your eyes from direct glare and the light is cast directly on the work surface without creating annoying, and dangerous, shadows that may interfere with your food preparation. It is essential to have this sort of unobstructed task lighting to allow you to see clearly as you work. Before you fix your lighting in place, you should also check that the pelmet protects you from glare when sitting at your table.

Halogen lighting is now available in a number of styles: in small tracks sprouting a number of bulbs, recessed or in single-fitting lamps. The bulbs are sold as spots, which cast a small pool of concentrated light, or wide angle, which shed larger pools with softer edges. Installing halogen is a specialist task as the lamps require transformers.

These are sold as small, heavy boxes or cigar-shaped tubes which transform the powerful mains into a low-voltage supply. Transformers can be fitted either close to the light source or remotely. They usually emit a slight hum and so are best placed inside the ceiling recess

or, perhaps, a cupboard. While manufacturers are making progress with this new technology, dimmer switches, as yet, rarely work successfully with low-voltage halogen. They can emit an incredibly annoying and ear-piercing whine.

Last, but by no means least, there are candles. Unless you are eccentric, these are not recommended for everyday lighting. However, for special occasions and romantic suppers, the diffused quality of candlelight is difficult to beat.

Flooring

Beautiful flooring really does make a huge difference to the room and you do not need to spend a fortune to achieve excellent results. Of course, if your budget is unlimited, you might like to lay stone or slate, but the chances are that you will have to be more realistic. Even where the purse is bottomless, you may not be able to fit some types of finishes, such as stone flags, ceramic and terracotta tiles, because your floor simply cannot take the weight.

If you do have a solid floor on which to work then the choices of finish are many and varied: limestone, granite, ceramic tiles, terracotta, wood, vinyl, cork or linoleum. The options open to those with timber floors are the lighter materials.

Your choice of colour and pattern is also important. A plain-colour floor, especially if it is white, will show every mark. Some small fleck or pattern will spare you hours of cleaning. That said, floors with a light-coloured base will brighten a room, while darker shades will close it in. Lively patterns can overwhelm a kitchen. A large room can look stunning with a bold black and white chequer-board design, but this treatment could completely swamp a small room. In smaller spaces, a plain finish is infinitely preferable. If in doubt, keep it simple.

Wood

If you are lucky enough to have good floorboards (most are hardwearing pine), this provides a wonderful opportunity to achieve a stripped and varnished finish at a reasonable cost. You could try a subtle pattern by choosing from some of the many colours of wood stain that are now available (see page 48). The advantages of timber are that it is durable, smart, warm and can improve with age. The disadvantages are that it can dent and scar if damaged by heavy or sharp objects, it is not particularly good at providing sound proofing and it requires some maintenance and occasional re-varnishing.

Cleaning up old floorboards is back-breaking and dusty work but the finished result is well worth the effort. You will probably need to replace some of the damaged boards and hire a professional sanding machine to lift off the worn and grubby top surface. If new boards are a lighter colour than your existing ones, you can 'age' them by painting on a couple of coats of cold, black tea. It is incredibly satisfying to see even the most filthy boards transformed as you pass the sander over them to reveal the pale, clean wood underneath. Once you have achieved an even surface and cleared away all the dust, paint the boards with several coats of tough varnish for a rich, glowing, warm and hardwearing finish. For a limed effect, paint the sanded boards with watered-down white emulsion and then protect with matte varnish. When painting or varnishing floors, make sure you start at the corner furthest from the door so that you do not find yourself trapped and have to walk across wet varnish to leave the room.

The rustic style of open wood beams, the heavy stone fireplace and pine furniture is complemented by the sturdy red brick flooring. This sort of porous material is difficult to keep spotlessly clean, but does collect a wonderful patina with age.

If all this sounds like too much effort, a good-quality wood finish is possible with the timber veneer and laminate packs available in every DIY store. The laminate finish is virtually indestructible. It resists damage from grit and sharp heels, stains and cigarette burns. These packs are sold in a variety of styles and colours, from prepared wood 'tiles' composed of small timber strips fixed on to a backing material, to lengths of tongue-and-groove. The tiles will give the effect of a parquet or wood-block floor, while the tongue-and-groove system resembles neat boards. These packs are sold either ready varnished or untreated so that you may stain and varnish them yourself.

Vinyl

This incredibly tough material is stain resistant, waterproof, easy to wash clean and warm to the touch. It is available in a wide range of thicknesses and prices. As a general rule of thumb, the thicker it is, the more it costs. Vinyl flooring is available either in sheets or tile form, cushioned or solid.

To achieve the best results with this material, it is essential to start with a well-prepared, flat base. Chipboard or hardboard are ideal. Using a recommended adhesive, both tiles and sheets are easy to lay and are virtually maintenance free.

Linoleum

This finish shares many of the properties of vinyl. It is warm, stain resistant, durable, easily washable, and is also available in sheet or tile form. In recent years, linoleum has enjoyed a revival of popularity because it is manufactured using natural materials: cork, linseed oil, wood and resins. As demand has increased, so has the choice of colours and patterns.

Cork Tiles

Easy to clean, warm under foot, inexpensive, tough, easy to lay and with an intriguing, mottled finish, cork has remained popular for years. It has the added advantage of being a natural material that is grown as a renewable material. As with wood and vinyl, the answer to a perfect finish lies in meticulous preparation. Cork tiles do not sit happily on uneven floors; they must be dry and flat. Spread the recommended adhesive over the entire surface of the tile to ensure a good, firm bond. Loose corners are easily damaged and will soon look ugly.

Tiles are sold ready prepared with a PVC coating or in their natural state. The natural tiles are slightly easier to cut and fit to awkward shapes and may be coloured with a stain either before or mixed in with the recommended varnish or sealant. Sealing is essential to ensure resistance to water penetration, stains from foods or drinks and for long life.

Ceramic Tiles

The ranges of ceramic floor tiles available expand almost daily. The choice includes hundreds of beautiful colours and patterns. They are hardwearing, easily cleaned and are available in all price ranges; not surprisingly, the best quality tiles are the most expensive. Their disadvantages are that they are hard, cold under foot, noisy and often slippery when wet. Almost without exception, they should be laid on solid floors, as they are likely to be too heavy to be laid on top of timber joists. For the very best results, especially in large areas, these tiles should be laid professionally.

Terracotta Tiles

There are few surfaces that look more gorgeous when well worn. Terracotta (baked clay) has a warm, red-brick colour that becomes wonderfully soft and muted with age. Because these tiles are heavy, they are best laid on solid floors.

Stone, Slate and Marble

For those with a large budget and solid floors, these finishes can look fabulous. Stone flags acquire a glorious patina with age, slate has a sleek, understated grandeur and marble can look incredibly luxurious. All are extremely hardwearing and expensive. They are also hard, cold and tend to be noisy. Because they are difficult to cut and lay, this work should be carried out by professionals.

Terrazzo

An aggregate composed of stone and glass chippings and concrete, this is tough, colourful, available in tiles or slabs and best laid on solid floors because of its heavy weight. Once again, it is worth paying an expert to fit this sort of flooring.

There are few floor coverings to beat the look of gorgeous, rich terracotta tiles. The large tiles featured here are reclaimed antique stock. They work extremely well with modern or traditional style units and while they are hard underfoot, they are fairly easy to keep clean.

The Professional Kitchen

For the enthusiastic amateur cook, it is always very exciting to watch a professional kitchen in full swing. It is like a stage bursting with drama as vegetables are washed and carefully prepared, sauces are seasoned and stirred, pastry is rolled, grills sizzle and oven doors are opened to unleash the most heavenly smells. And all of this carefully choreographed activity is set against a backdrop of sleek stainless steel and glistening tiles.

The room is a machine for cooking and it is designed to work with the efficiency and precision of an engine. The professional kitchen must withstand tremendous amounts of wear and tear, it must be highly functional and, above all, it must be hygienic and easy to clean.

With the growing interest in cooking and experimenting with international cuisine, the amateur cook has become increasingly adventurous. And what better place to put your skills to work than your own professional-style kitchen?

The Ingredients

The colour palette is minimal and based around silver, grey, black and white. You might, however, choose to soften the effect slightly by adding a splash of bold colour. Select from cobalt blue, grass green, egg-yolk yellow, pillar-box red or terracotta. Use one of these colours for accessories: the telephone, chairs, stools, crockery, a band of tiles, a waste bin, a huge fruit bowl, tea towels, and so on. If you are feeling bold, use one of these colours on the walls.

Together with basic colours, the professional kitchen is distinguished by the exciting combination of subtle textures and finishes. Among the essential ingredients are simple, smooth surfaces, stainless steel, aluminium, chrome, tin, timber, plain white, grey or black ceramic tiles, glass, and, for an extra flourish you could incorporate marble or slate.

The Recipe

The beauty and elegance of this kitchen springs from its emphasis on functionalism.

Surfaces of floors, walls, units and work tops must be cleared of obstructions and easy to clean. Most professional kitchens opt for non-slip ceramic tiling on floors largely because it is hardwearing, stain resistant and easy to clean.

If you are aiming for the full, high-tech look, investigate the possibility of laying down sheet aluminium. This is intended for use as industrial flooring and is extremely tough and surprisingly inexpensive. Its greatest virtue is that it can cover up all manner of ills, especially uneven and damaged floors, and always looks dazzling. Because the sheet material requires special cutting tools, it is worthwhile paying for a professional fitter.

With the ever-growing interest in food and cooking, the professional kitchen has provided a source of design inspiration for the amateur. There is, of course, a great deal we can learn from the professional — not only are the cooking skills of the highest calibre, so are the standards of cleanliness and efficiency.

If you find the thought of ceramic or aluminium too harsh when combined with large areas of stainless steel, there are plenty of other flooring options. For example, in a domestic setting, there are few combinations to beat a good, varnished wooden floor and stainless steel or grey-coloured units. Linoleum and vinyl would look smart too - especially those incorporating a slight fleck.

If your budget cannot stretch to stainless steel units, take a look at a tough, smooth laminate finish, available in whites, greys and silvers. Painted finishes look good too - why not try a matte-finish pewter colour on wood, or transform old laminate doors with a metallic-effect paint. Stainless steel or aluminium handles and door knobs complete the effect.

Additional storage space can be provided by free-standing, industrial, stainless steel shelving units, stainless steel hanging rails (excellent for saucepans and cooking utensils) and, perhaps, stainless steel or glass wall-fixed shelves.

The classic professional work surface is sheet stainless steel. This acquires a soft patina with age and wear and tear - it will scratch but that adds to its charm. Industrial kitchen suppliers will be able to put you in contact with specialist fitters. For less expensive options consider a simple white or grey laminate. A small slab of grey or white marble adds the professional touch - all the best chefs use marble for rolling out pastry.

Walls can be simply tiled in white, painted white or clad in sheet steel. Fixing stainless steel panels is very easy (see pages 46-7) and they look very stylish above a cooker or sink where they perform as the perfect splash back.

Stainless steel appliances can be hard to find and can also be expensive. A steel hob will be no problem. However, unless you have a budget that will stretch to professional cookers, you may find it more difficult to find a shiny oven. Do not despair; a smart white oven should look perfectly at home with the rest of your scheme.

Items such as dishwashers, refrigerators, and washing machines with doors can have their fronts disguised with fine-gauge stainless steel panels. These are easily secured in place with the appropriate adhesive. Sinks, of course, present no problem at all - the vast majority available on the domestic market are made of stainless steel. Industrial ones are more expensive, but are unusually large. The choice of taps is enormous - you are sure to be able to find exactly what you want.

Finishing Touches

There is a vast array of intriguing and useful objects that will complete the professional style of your kitchen.

A stainless steel trolley is an extremely handy item, not just for wheeling dishes between kitchen and dining room but

also for everyday storage. Trolleys look great piled high with stainless steel saucepans, casserole pots, cheese graters, coffee pots, trays and serving dishes.

A small galvanised dustbin makes a practical, handsome and inexpensive waste bin; stainless steel mixing bowls and colanders are good for displaying fruit. Chrome-finish clocks are easy to find.

Happy cooking.

The sleek finish of stainless steel looks great, is long lasting and, because there are few dirt traps, is easy to keep looking fresh.

(Left) Professional stainless steel accessories, such as this practical hanging rail, bring a sense of order to the kitchen and keep utensils safely but within easy reach.

Project 1:
• • • • • • • • •

Tiling the wall behind your work surface

Tiling a small area like this is possible even for the least experienced at 'do-it-yourself' – and, with a little patience and care, the results will look excellent.

The key to success is good preparation. Before starting work make sure you have all the materials and tools to hand and the time necessary to complete the job.

Measure the space to be tiled to estimate the number of tiles you will need. It is always a good idea to buy a few spares just in case you break a couple while fixing them, or in case of later damage when you may need replacements.

When buying the adhesive and grout, read the instructions carefully to make sure you have the right type and the correct quantity. If in doubt, ask; all good hardware shops will be able to offer advice.

Tools and Materials

- two wood battens, about 3 x 12mm (½ in) and long enough to frame one side and the length of area to be tiled
- spirit level
- small nails or pins
- adhesive (check that the pack includes a spreader)
- tiles (as estimated, plus a few spare)
- pack of tile spacers
- tile cutter
- water-resistant grout

1 Ensure the area of wall to be tiled is sound and smooth. Remove all traces of old wallpaper or old tiles, chip off any loose paint or wall plaster. If necessary, fill cracks and holes with a plaster filler and smooth with sandpaper.

2 Using a pencil and the wood battens, mark out the area to be tiled. Draw a grid on the wall of tile positions, leaving grouting space of around 3mm (⅛ in) between each tile. An important consideration here is that the top row is composed of whole tiles; cut tiles along the top will look messy. Use the spirit level to ensure the lines are level. Using small nails or pins, fix one of the battens along the lowest horizontal line. The tiling between this batten and the work surface will be completed at the end of the job. Fixing a vertical batten is also a good idea to keep the lines straight. Both battens will be removed when the job is complete.

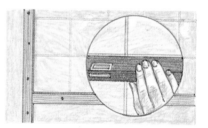

3 Most tile adhesive is sold with a spreader (a flat piece of plastic with one notched edge) inside the pack. Use this tool to spread adhesive directly on to the wall - this usually needs to be around 3mm (⅛ in) deep, but check directions for recommended thickness. When you are tiling a large area, apply adhesive in sections of around 1 square metre (9 square ft) at a time.

4 Lay the first tile at the right-angled corner made by the two battens. Press firmly into place. Continue along the horizontal line, using spacers between each tile. Check that the tiles in the first row have stuck well before starting on the line above. Continue until the whole area is tiled.

5 Allow to dry for a day before filling tile gaps with grout. Ensure that the grout is pressed firmly into the gaps and remove any excess with a damp cloth. Once the grout has dried, prise off the battens and fill any holes made by the pins. Finish the job by completing the last line of tiling and grouting.

Project 2:
· · · · · · · · · ·

An easy splashback

Stainless steel provides a simple, smart and surprisingly inexpensive solution as a cooker splash back. It can be used to disguise an uneven wall or unsightly tiles and is easy to fix and to keep clean. The final results have a truly professional look.

Measure the area to be covered by the splash back. If the sheet is intended to fit in a recessed area, then pay special attention to the shape of the corners. If they are not perfectly square, the sheet of steel may have to be cut in such a way that takes this into account. If you have any doubts about the measuring, it is a good idea to make a cardboard cut-out in the shape to be covered by steel. Take the measurements and/or the cut-out to the supplier who will cut the metal to shape. It is also a good idea to ask the supplier to drill the sheet with fixing holes. The best sheet steel is sold covered with a thin plastic film. This is peeled off as you fix the sheet to the wall.

Tools and Materials

- stainless steel (as estimated)
- electric or hand drill with a masonry bit
- rawl plugs
- mirror screws or screws with press-on metal caps
- screwdriver

1 To ensure the sheet fits perfectly, hold it in place. If any additional trimming is

required, return to the supplier. This is a specialised task requiring specialised tools; if you attempt this yourself you could end up spoiling the metal.

2 Take the sheet of steel, with the plastic film side facing you, and hold in place. Mark where you need to drill holes in the wall.

3 Remove the steel and drill the holes in the wall to the depth of the screws. Push rawl plugs into the drilled holes. Hold up the sheet of steel again and peel back the protective plastic film from around the top, central hole where you fix the first screw. You can now let go of the sheet.

4 Continuing at the top of the sheet, peel back the plastic film round the next screws and fix. Continue to peel down the plastic as you screw the sheet of steel in place. As you reach the last screw you can remove the plastic altogether.

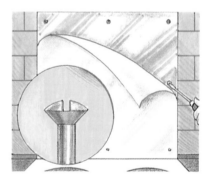

Project 3:
• • • • • • • • • •

Painting a wood floor

Wooden floors have tremendous charm and, when carefully maintained, will improve with age. The timber finishes available are many and varied, from natural, waxed wood to varnished, stained and painted boards.

Before you start, ensure the wood surface is smooth and grit, grease and dust free. Remove all nails. If the floor has recently been uncovered, you may need to level the surface and clean it up with a professional sanding machine - available from most DIY hire shops.

Measure up the room and draw a floor plan marking in the fixed units - it is a good idea to do this on graph paper. Decide on the floor pattern, in this case a light and dark check, and draw it on the floor plan. As a general rule, larger patterns suit larger rooms. If you have a spacious kitchen, tiles can be as large as 35cm (14 in) square; for small rooms try for around 20cm (8 in) square.

Tools and Materials

- long batten (to help you draw straight lines)
- ruler
- masking tape
- light and dark wood stain or paint
- paint brush
- sandpaper
- clear varnish

1 Transfer the pattern to the floor with pencil lines.

2 Place masking tape round the edges of the light areas and paint on the light stain. You will achieve a much more professional finish by applying two thin layers rather than one thick one.

Leave to dry. Apply the coats of stain until you achieve the depth of stain you require. When dry, remove the masking tape.

3 Now mask the dark areas and paint on the stain. Be extremely careful at the edges and do not to let the dark stain run into the light areas. Leave to dry, then remove the tape.

4 Lightly sand, by hand, the entire floor surface to ensure a good smooth finish. Brush away all dust and add two or three coats of varnish to seal the surface.

Project 4:
· · · · · · · · ·
Storage shelving

In almost every kitchen there is a small gap where units have not quite stretched from wall to wall. These gaps can provide extremely useful storage space. At base-unit level they are ideal for items such as large trays or perhaps a small wine rack; at eye level they are great for books and compact discs or tapes.

Measure the space available and make a rough sketch of the unit you plan to make. This unit can be made in a variety of materials; plywood or pine are among the easiest to work with.

Tools and Materials

- plywood, pine or chosen material (as estimated)
- ruler
- wood adhesive
- small screws and nails
- hammer
- screwdriver

1 Essentially, this shelf unit is a simple box with two shelves. Take one long side piece and fix on to it the top and bottom pieces. These should be glued and screwed or nailed into place. Then fix the remaining side and, finally, the back panel.

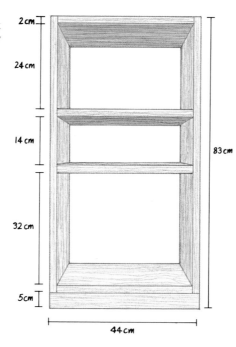

2 Measure the largest cookery book and the size of a compact disc (or tape) pack. Your largest books will fit on the bottom shelf, so mark the height of the tallest book on the side of the unit: this will determine where you fix the shelves. Leave a 12mm-2cm (½-¾ in) gap between the top of the book and bottom of the shelf. Then, allowing for the width of the shelf, the compact disc (or tape) pack and a small gap, mark where the next shelf will go.

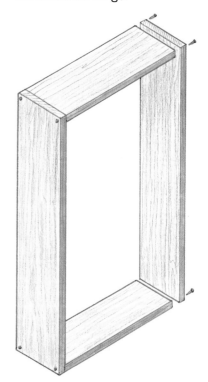

3 With the unit on its back, slot in the shelves to ensure they fit well. Slot in the tallest book and a compact disc (or tape) pack, too, to make sure the measuring has been accurate.

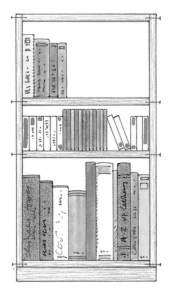

4 Fix the shelves in place using wood adhesive and small screws driven into the shelf end from the outside of the panel. Careful measuring will ensure accuracy. Your new shelf unit is now ready for painting or varnishing.

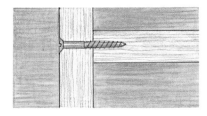

Project 5:
· · · · · · · · ·

Painted doors

If you have old kitchen units that are sturdy and serviceable, but you dislike the exisiting doors, painting on your own designs or using stencils can give them a new lease of life. The paint effects can be as simple or complex as you like, but remember that the simplest patterns are often the most effective.

Tools and Materials

- several sheets of rough paper to test designs
- some stiff cardboard from which you can cut a template
- pencil and ruler
- abrasive paper
- methylated spirit
- one fine and one 12 mm (½ in) paintbrush
- stencil
- stencil brush
- masking tape
- stencil paint or primer and gloss or eggshell

2 Paint on a coat of primer. This will help the finish coats to adhere well. Leave to dry.

3 Rub over the units once again with fine abrasive paper to remove all specs of dust and grit. Add the base coat of paint and leave to dry.

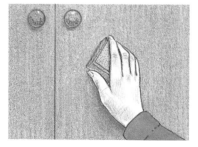

4 If you are adding a stencilled pattern, mark the stencil positions in pencil on the doors and check that you are happy with the layout.

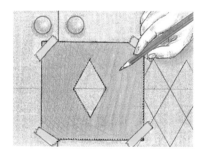

5 If you have chosen to design your own pattern you'll need to make a cardboard template. The template can, of course, be almost any shape or size, but remember that bold, simple designs, such as the geometric one shown, work extremely well. The harlequin diamond pattern in

1 Thoroughly wash the areas to be painted to remove all traces of grease and grubby fingermarks. When dry, rub over the surface with abrasive paper to prime the surface and provide a key for the paint finish. Brush away any dust and, using a cloth dampened with methylated spirit, wipe down the units.

our picture was created as follows. First, the door was measured and the size of diamond decided. The template was cut, held in place on the door at regular intervals and drawn round in pencil to form the outline of the pattern.

6 Apply the contrasting colour using the stencil or by filling in the guidelines drawn on the doors. Take care not to load the brush too heavily as this may cause the paint to run or spatter. Leave to dry thoroughly.

Project 6:
• • • • • • • • •

Patterning kitchen tiles

This is a quick and simple way of brightening up plain tiles. A strong geometric pattern is easy to achieve and can look stunning or, for something more unusual, you can produce the cut-out effect in our picture based on kitchen utensils and cutlery.

You will need to gather the chosen utensils, cutlery and so on and ensure that the tiles are clean and free from grease.

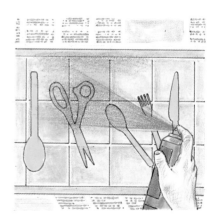

Tools and Materials

- several sheets of card or stiff paper
- scissors
- double-sided sticky tape
- masking tape
- old newspapers
- aerosol can of car spray paint in the chosen colour
- paint brush
- small can of clear varnish

Remember, when using the aerosol, it is very important to leave doors and windows open for plenty of ventilation.

4 Spray the tile area. Leave to dry. Check instructions on the can to see how long the manufacturer suggests for drying.

1 On the card or paper, draw round the cutlery and utensils; a corkscrew, wooden spoon, scissors and so on. Cut out these shapes.

2 Design a pattern with the cut-out shapes and, using the double-sided tape, stick the pieces in place on to the tiles.

3 With masking tape and old newspaper, mask off the area around the tiles. On a piece of newspaper, try a few practice strokes of paint spray to get used to using the aerosol. It is usually best to hold the nozzle around 25cm (10 in) away from the surface to ensure an even coverage.

5 Once the paint is dry, peel off the cut-outs. Seal the surface with a coat of clear varnish.

Project 7:
. . . .

Decorative panels for unit doors

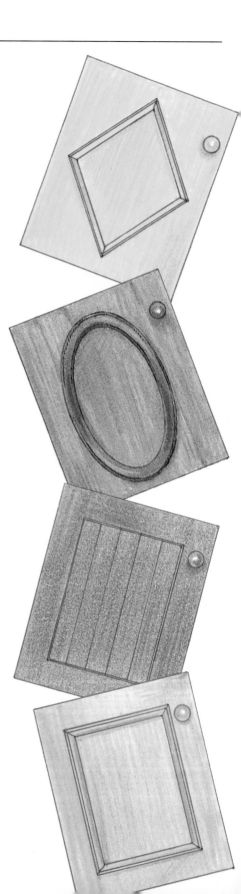

There are many ways to give your kitchen a face lift and improve the look of old units. Adding a coat of paint or stencilling on patterns are among the options, but you may also like to add decorative panelling. Panelling kits are now widely available in hardware stores and they are inexpensive and easy to fit. Make sure that you measure the doors carefully before buying your kit.

If you cannot find the right kit, it is easy to make the panels for yourself from the mouldings sold in timer suppliers and hardware stores. To make these, you will need the length of the chosen moulding, a saw and a mitre box - the box enables you to saw accurate corners. Measure the size of panel required, cut wood to length then pin with panel pins and glue for extra strength.

Before you begin, ensure the doors are clean and free from all grease. Use washing up liquid or little neat vinegar on stubborn grease marks.

Tools and Materials

- panelling kit or the own home-made panels (see above)
- spirit level
- adhesive (if not supplied in the kit)

1 Using a pencil, mark the position of the panels on the doors. Take great care to make sure the lines are level - use a spirit level if you are unsure.

2 Hold the panels in place to make sure that they look right. The adhesive used in most kits is already applied to the underside of the panels; all you need to do is peel off the protective backing strip. If you are sticking on your own panels, draw a thin line of wood adhesive on the back of the panels.

3 With the adhesive exposed, place the panels against the door and manoeuvre into place. Press firmly to fix. Leave to bond and dry.

56

Project 8:
• • • • • • • • • •

A saucepan rack

This is a useful way of storing bulky items like saucepans, while also keeping them within easy reach. A number of manufacturers produce a variety of racks, but it's also possible to make your own using a chrome or stainless steel wardrobe rail.

Select the most convenient area for the rack and check that the wall is sound and will have the strength to carry the weight of a number of saucepans. Walls constructed of brick and plaster are ideal. Thin wood or plasterboard partitions will not be able to support the weight.

Tools and Materials

- 2 rail supports
- metal tubing cut to the required length
- electric or hand drill
- rawl plugs
- screws
- metal butcher's hooks

2 Drill the holes and push in rawl plugs. Screw the first rail support into place. Slot in the rail, then fix the second support.

3 Rest butcher's hooks on the rail and hang the saucepans.

1 Hold up the rail and rail supports and, with a pencil, mark the places where you will need to drill holes. Remove the rail and supports.

Storing recyclable materials

Wth the growing interest in recycling household waste material comes the need to store it neatly. If your aim is to be environment friendly, it is a good idea to start with your own environment and keep that clean and tidy.

This rack is designed to take three waste materials: glass, newspapers and cans. It can stand on its end while it is being filled and then tipped up to form a carrying crate to dispose of the waste.

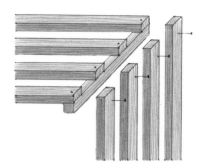

3 Nail and glue together the two sections. You now have the skeleton of the crate. When the glue is dry, nail and glue on the back panel of plywood.

Tools and Materials

- saw
- 8 x 36cm (14 ⅜ in) lengths of 20 x 20mm (¾ x ¾ in) timber
- 8 x 30cm (12 in) lengths of 35 x 10mm (1 ¾ x ½ in) timber
- 8 x 56cm (22 ¾ in) lengths of 35 x 10mm (1 ¾ x ½ in) timber
- 1 piece 5mm (¼ in) plywood, 56 x 33cm (22 ¾ x 1 ¾ in)
- 2 pieces 5mm (¼ in) plywood, 36 x 30cm (14 ⅜ x 12 in)
- 20mm (¾ in) nails
- hammer
- wood glue

1 Take two lengths of 20 x 20mm (¾ x ¾ in) timber and, at equal distances, nail and glue on four 300cm (12 in) lengths of 35 x 10mm (1 ¾ x ½ in) timber. Repeat the exercise. This will make the top and bottom sections.

2 Take one of the sections and, at equal intervals, nail and glue on to the 20 x 20mm (¾ x ¾ in) timber and four 56cm (22 ¾ in) lengths of 35 x 10mm (1 ¾ x ½ in) timber. Repeat the exercise. You now have a top and side section and a bottom and side section.

4 To fix the shelves, nail and glue the four remaining 20 x 20mm (¾ x ¾ in) timbers to the two side panels to form rests for the shelves. Leave for the glue to set.

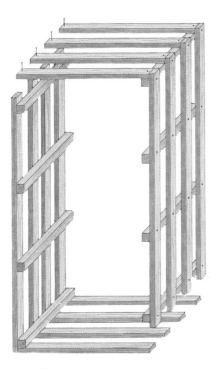

5 Slide the ply shelves into place, glue and nail.

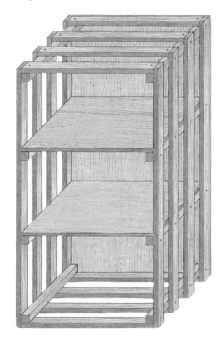

Project 10:

• • • • • • • • • •

New handles

Old or damaged handles can make doors and drawers difficult to open - and they look scruffy. New ones can give a kitchen a real lift. Select the new handles with care, ensuring they are in a finish that matches your decor; brass handles, for example, look odd next to stainless steel taps, and very ornate Victorian handles will sit uncomfortably in a modern-style room.

Tools and Materials

- ruler
- length of wood or long rule
- required number of new handles
- suitable screws and fittings, if not supplied with handles
- screwdriver

1 Remove the old handles carefully, taking care not to cause damage. It may be that the new handles are of a completely different type from the existing ones, in which case you will need to fill the old holes with an appropriate filler and very carefully drill new ones.

2 Take great care in measuring for new holes; if handles are out of alignment on a drawer unit they will look very messy. Use a pencil to mark clearly where the handles are to be fixed and, using a length of wood or long rule, ensure they line up perfectly.

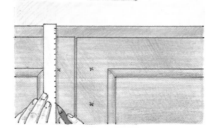

3 Fix new handles according to the manufacturer's instructions.

Index

appliances 12, 23, 28-33, 43
architectural details 18

broom cupboard 14, 22

candles 35
ceramic tiles 12, 22, 24, 38, 40, 54-5
children 10, 23
colour schemes 12, 22, 26, 40
cooker 10, 12, 18, 28-30
cooker hood 30
cork tiles 38
counter 16
cupboards 21-2

decor panels 31, 33
decoration 24-6
dimmer switch 35
dining area 22, 24-6
disability 10-12, 14, 30
dishwasher 10, 31-3, 43
doors, cupboard 12, 22, 52-3, 56-7
doorway 8, 12, 14, 18, 23
dresser 21

elderly 10, 30
electric cooker 12, 28, 30
electric sockets 23
extractor fan 16, 30

finishes 12, 22, 24-6, 30, 40
fire precautions 23
fitted kitchen 12, 21, 30
flooring 12, 36-9, 40-2
fluorescent lighting 34, 35
freezer 31
furniture 21

galley kitchen 16
gas cooker 12, 28, 30

halogen lighting 34, 35
handles, replacing 62-3
hanging rails 21, 23, 42, 58-9
height problems 14, 18

high-tech look 40-3
hob 28-30, 43

island kitchen 10, 16-17

kitchen-in-a-box unit 8

L-shaped kitchen 14-16
laminate 12, 22, 42
large kitchen 10
layout 10, 14-18, 30
light, natural 8, 26
lighting 12, 23, 34-5
line kitchen 16
linoleum 38, 42

marble 39, 42
medium-sized kitchen 8
microwave oven 10, 28, 30

oven 12, 28-30, 43

paint 24, 26, 42
painting wood floors 48-9
painting doors 52-3
panelling 26, 56-7
patterning tiles 54-5
pendant lighting 34
perspex 26
plan, drawing 8
plate rack 21
plumbing 10, 16, 33

recessed lighting 35
refrigerator 10, 18, 31, 43
rise-and-fall lamp 35
room size 8-10

safety 23, 30
saucepan rack 58-9
shelf unit 50-1
shelving 21, 22, 42
sink 10, 12, 14, 18, 33, 43
small kitchen 8
splashback, fixing 46

stainless steel 21, 22, 26, 30, 33, 42-3, 46-7
stencilling 24, 52
stippling 24
stone 12, 22-3, 39
storage 10, 12, 21-2, 42, 60-1
stripped floorboards 36
structural work 8, 18
style 12

table 10, 16, 18, 22
taps 33, 43
terracotta tiles 38
terrazzo 12, 39
texture 22, 40
themes 26
tiling a wall 44-5
track lighting 35
trolley 21, 43
tumble dryer 33
tungsten lights 34

U-shaped kitchen 14
unfitted kitchen 12, 21
units 12, 14, 42
uplighters 35
use of kitchen 10-12

ventilation 23
vinyl flooring 38, 42

wall coverings 12, 24-6
wall lights 34-5
wallpaper 24-6
washing machine 33, 43
waste bin 43
waste chute 33
waste disposal unit 33
waste recycling rack 60-1
windows 8, 10, 18
wood 12, 22
wooden flooring 36-8, 42, 48-9
wooden panelling 26
work tops 12, 22, 42
work triangle 18